Easy & Fun
Paper Folding

This book belongs to

Grandma

©Disney

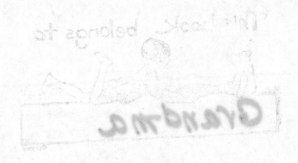

Easy & Fun
Paper Folding

Johanna Huber and Christel Claudius

Sterling Publishing Co., Inc.   New York

Translation by
Elisabeth E. Reinersmann

Translation edited and layout designed by
Rodman Pilgrim Neumann

Drawings and photographs by
Christel Claudius

Library of Congress Cataloging-in-Publication Data

Huber, Johanna.
  [Lustiges Papierfaltbüchlein. English]
  Easy and fun paper folding / Johanna Huber, Christel Claudius.
    p.   cm.
  Translation of: Lustiges Papierfaltbüchlein.
  1. Origami.   I. Claudius, Christel.   II. Title.
TT870.H8313   1990
736'.982—dc20   90–9829
                                                          CIP

10 9 8 7 6 5 4 3 2 1

English translation © 1990 by Sterling Publishing Company
387 Park Avenue South, New York, N.Y. 10016
Original edition published under the title
Lustiges Papierfaltbüchlein
© 1988 by Ravensburger Buchverlag Otto Maler GmbH
Distributed in Canada by Sterling Publishing
% Canadian Manda Group, P.O. Box 920, Station U
Toronto, Ontario, Canada M8Z 5P9
Distributed in Great Britain and Europe by Cassell PLC
Villiers House, 41/47 Strand, London WC2N 5JE, England
Distributed in Australia by Capricorn Ltd.
P.O. Box 665, Lane Cove, NSW 2066
Manufactured in the United States of America
All rights reserved
Sterling ISBN 0–8069–7444–3

CONTENTS

INTRODUCTION

Paperfolding is a fascinating, fun-filled, and creative activity for children—as well as adults. With a minimum of folds and creases they can transform a flat piece of paper into a three-dimensional form like a house, a pinwheel, a boat or even a hat. This activity encourages children to experiment, and it is wonderful practice for developing manual dexterity as well as patience and exactness.

Children benefit from the guidance of an adult during this activity. It is therefore a perfect opportunity for spending playful time together.

With this book we are incorporating many well-known traditional and easy-to-execute paperfolding methods such as those designed by the educator Friedrich Froebel. The degree of difficulty is carefully arranged from the easier to the more complex forms. Some of the latter may even be fun for adults who either like a little challenge or just want to relax.

To assure that every project will turn out as described, a diagram accompanies each step of the folding process. Practise the basic forms first. Build on this experience before attempting to do the more difficult figures. Once you have mastered the basic concept it will be fun to do the more complicated forms. And who knows, your next adventure might well be more-advanced origami. Also, use your imagination after you have carefully followed all instructions at least once, and try to design your own creations. Now you can begin your Easy and Fun Paper Folding.

——Johanna Huber
Christel Claudius

Basic Rules

Before you begin, take note of the following rules.

1. Work on a hard, smooth and flat surface, so that all folds and creases can be executed with accuracy.
2. It is important to make each fold precisely as described *and* to move your thumbnail sharply over that fold for exactness. Each subsequent step is then made easier to execute, and the stability of the finished form is increased as well.
3. Study each step and corresponding diagram before you start folding the paper. This will give you a mental picture of the sequence of steps you are about to do. It is useful—while you execute a fold—to picture in your mind's eye the step that follows and to remember the one just completed.
4. If you use colored paper, make sure the colored side is face down on the table at the beginning of your folding.

Every finished figure is a combination of a set of basic forms, and every one is clearly demonstrated. The basic forms consist of only a few simple folds that are not difficult to execute. With some additional folding they are easily developed into more elaborate figures.

Some of the terminology used in the step-by-step descriptions are explained below.

Crease:	a fold that is opened up again.
Line:	a line connecting two points.
Open up:	unfold a fold just made.
Turn:	the side of the paper (or form) facing you is turned face down.
Turning:	move the form to a different direction (rotate) without lifting it off the table.
Fold over:	to fold a crease backwards.

THE SQUARE

Almost all of the figures in this book begin with a square piece of paper, for instance the tent, the pinwheel, the boat, the wallet, the different boxes and baskets, many of the animals, and even the salt-and-pepper dish or "fortune teller."

It is convenient to use origami paper, which comes precut into squares in three sizes and in 12 different colors. One type of origami paper is rather firm with a shiny coating on one side. The other is softer and of uniform color. Choose the paper best suited for the figure you want to do, but remember that many other papers—not only

origami paper—can be used. Any paper that can withstand repeated folding without stretching or tearing is fine, such as typewriter paper, paper from magazines, or gift-wrap paper.

Just make sure that you remember the basic requirement: the square you start out with must be a *true* square. It is very easy to make a true square out of a rectangular piece of paper by folding one corner diagonally upwards to the opposite edge of the paper. This produces a perfect right angle. The excess paper is then carefully trimmed off. And you have the square.

THE STRAIGHT CROSS

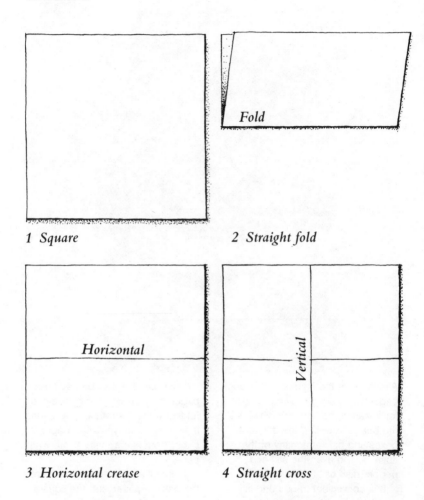

1 *Square*

2 *Straight fold*

Fold

3 *Horizontal crease*

Horizontal

4 *Straight cross*

Vertical

1. Take up both lower corners with the thumb and index finger of each hand, and...
2. ...fold upwards until they meet the upper corners. Press the fold with your thumbnail.
3. Unfold the paper. This is a "horizontal crease," but it can of

course become a vertical crease if the paper is folded from left to right.
4. Make a horizontal crease, and then turn the paper so that a second horizontal crease can be made to complete the straight cross.

THE DIAGONAL CROSS

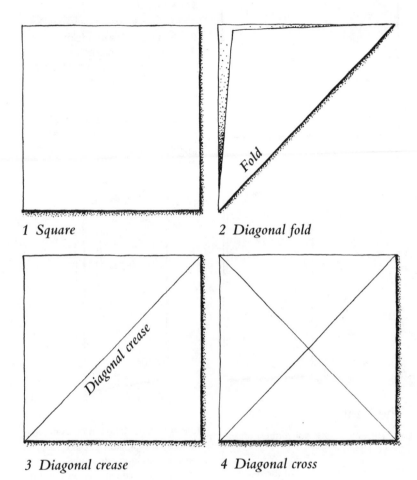

1 Square

2 Diagonal fold

3 Diagonal crease

4 Diagonal cross

1. Take up the lower right corner with your thumb and index finger, and . . .
2. . . . position the paper so that it will meet the upper left corner. Press the fold with your thumbnail.
3. Open the paper up again. This is a "diagonal crease."
4. Repeat the same procedure with the opposite corner in order to complete the diagonal cross.

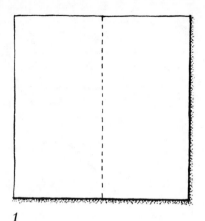

1

Here you can create with just one fold a few fun things to play with!

The Book

1. Fold a square in half vertically . . .
2. . . . and you have a folder.
3. Take a few more squares— folded in half—and held together with a string—and you have a book.

You might want to paste a label on the front. You can use it as a picture album or you can write or draw in it.

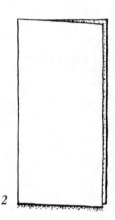

2

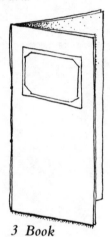

3 Book

The Tent

4. Turn the folder horizontally and you have a tent.

If you line up a few of these, you have a tunnel. It's fun to use the tunnel to hide things in or to move things through like pencils or toy cars; it also lends itself well to shooting marbles in one end and out the other.

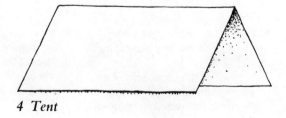

4 Tent

The Scarf

5. Fold a square diagonally...
6. ...and you have a scarf.

Decorate your scarf with a contrasting color border, or cut partially into the edges along the square sides to create fringes. Now you can use your colorful fringed scarf to dress up a favorite doll.

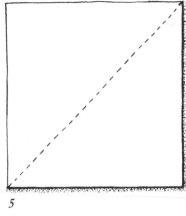

5

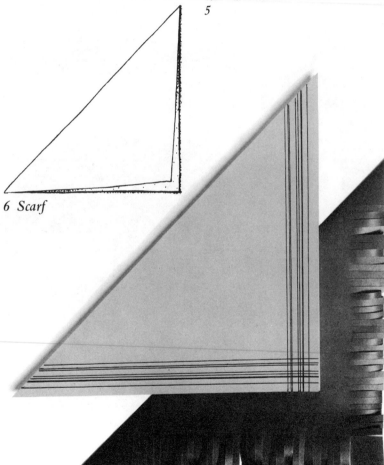

6 Scarf

Hidden in a square piece of paper is a whole house!

The House

1. Fold a square in half horizontally...
2. ...with the fold along the top.
3. Crease the form along the middle...
4. ...and fold both upper corners down towards the middle.

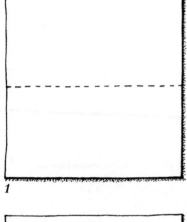

1

2

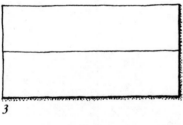

3

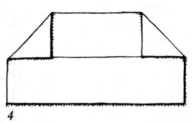

4

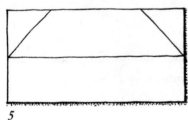

5

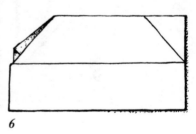

6

7 *House*

5. Open up the form.
6. Fold over all creases, except the very first which is the roofline, and fold the corners inside as shown.
7. Now draw windows and doors on your house.

BASIC FORM I

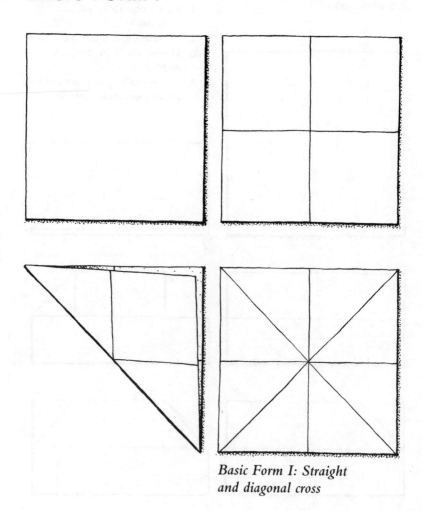

Basic Form I: Straight and diagonal cross

The Straight and Diagonal Cross

Begin by making the creases for the straight cross. Follow these by making the creases that give the diagonal cross. This gives Basic Form I, which is the basis for many subsequent forms.

NET I

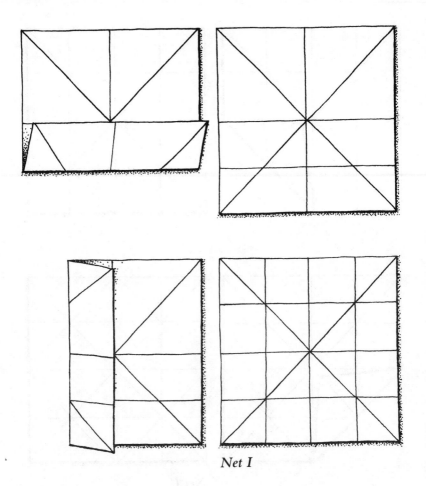

Net I

The square that has been creased according to the instructions on the previous page—Basic Form I—should be lifted with thumb and index finger on both lower corners, and the lower edge folded precisely against the horizontal crease. Make sure this crease is executed with

exactness by pressing your thumbnail along the fold. Unfold the paper and repeat the same step with each of the other edges. This procedure yields Net I, which is—again—a basic form for many projects.

17

NET II

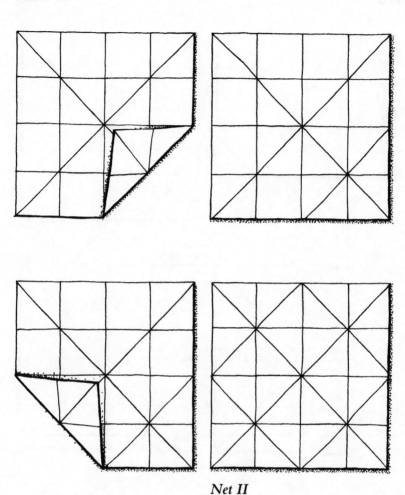

Net II

The paper you have creased to give Net I is taken at the lower right corner and folded diagonally up to meet the center point of the square.

Sharpen this crease, unfold and repeat the same step with the other corners. This is Net II.

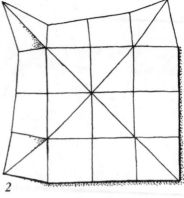

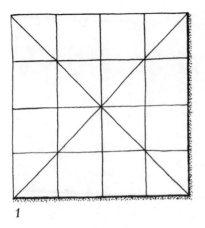

Net I can become a table.

Table

1. Make the necessary creases for Net I.
2. Fold each corner together into a point . . .
3. . . . and fold each triangle you have formed sideways as shown.
4. Realign the points along the diagonals and you have a table.

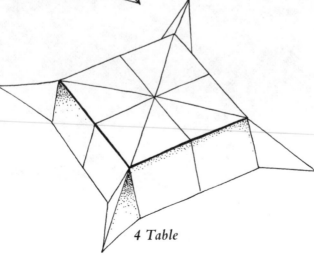

4 Table

19

The Pinwheel

The folding sequence for the windmill yields a basic form for many other projects.

1. Crease a square to make Net II (see page 18). The two sides marked A——A and B——B...
2. ...are folded inside to meet their respective midline crease. The lower left corner will form a triangle that is folded on its side...
3. ...and is called a "wing." Turn your form so that you can...

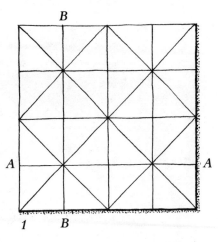

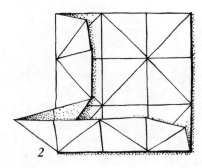

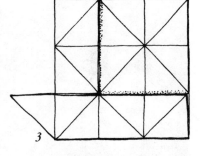

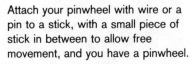

4. ...do the same procedure with the remaining sides...
5. ...until you have four wings.

Attach your pinwheel with wire or a pin to a stick, with a small piece of stick in between to allow free movement, and you have a pinwheel.

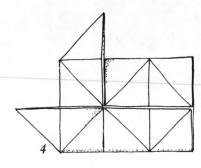

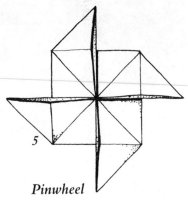

Pinwheel

Flounder

1. Crease a square to make the starting form, Net II...
2. ...continue folding to make a pinwheel (see page 21).
3. Fold wing A upwards toward the midline as shown, and fold wing B to the diagonal line.
4. Turn form. Pull out wing C, unfolding that side of the form so that corners D and E can be folded backwards.
5. This is your flounder.

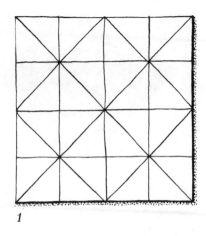

1

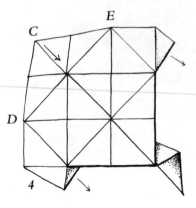

2

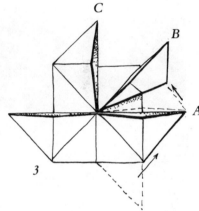

3

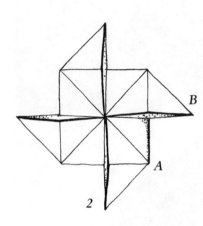

4

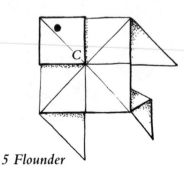

5 Flounder

Vase

1. Fold a pinwheel (see page 21).
2. Fold the pinwheel in half backwards along its diagonal axis . . .
3. . . . and by turning the form slightly your vase is finished.

Boat

4. Fold point A of the vase diagonally towards point B.
5. There you have a small boat with a sail.

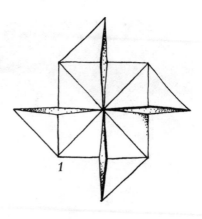

1

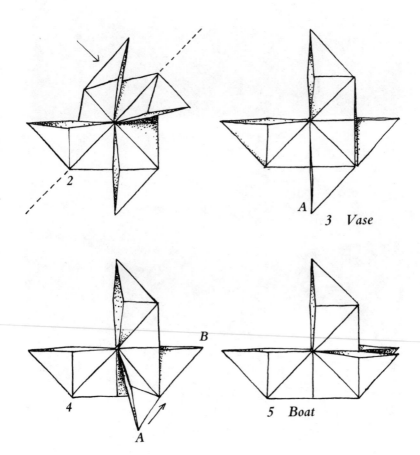

2

3 *Vase*

4

5 *Boat*

Bird

1. Fold the vase (see page 25).
2. Point A is folded back towards point B. Point C is folded towards the right on the diagonal crease, which requires that the form be opened up slightly.
3. The last step gives you the head, which only needs a pair of eyes to complete the bird with wings.

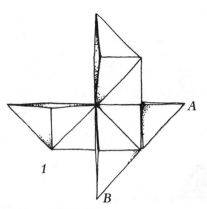

1

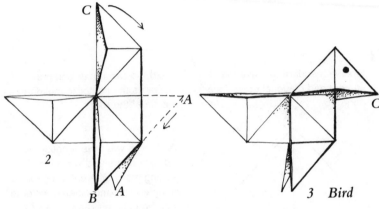

2

3 Bird

Duck

4. Points A and B are folded inside along the horizontal line.
5. And here you have a duck swimming in the pond.

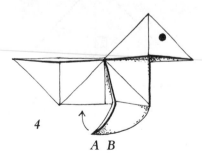

4

A B

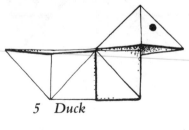

5 Duck

27

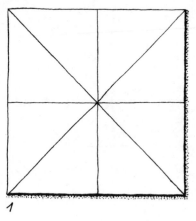

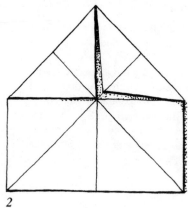

Houses

1. Crease a square to make the straight and diagonal cross (see page 16).

2. Fold the two upper corners towards the center to make the angle of the roof.

And there you have a house. All it needs are doors and windows. By choosing many different sizes for the starting square and different colored paper, you can build a whole village.

Houses

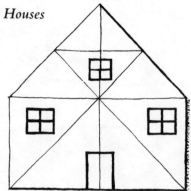

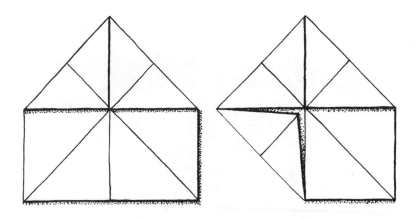

Envelope

If you fold one more of the corners of the house towards the middle, you will have an envelope. Use adhesive tape to hold the folds together, and add a bright lively stamp along with the address.

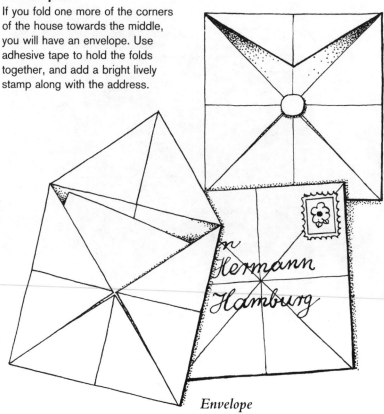

Envelope

BASIC FORM II

1. Crease a square to make the straight and diagonal cross, Basic Form I (see page 16).
2. Fold all four corners towards the middle.
3. Turn form and repeat the same procedure, folding the four new corners to the middle.
4. This is Basic Form II.

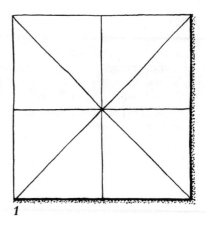

1

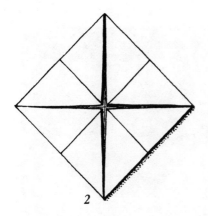

2

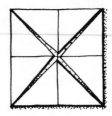

3

On the opposite page the photo shows the front and the back of Basic Form II. The top shows the back—corresponding to diagram 4—and the lower shows the front view.

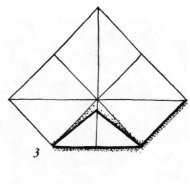

4 Back view,
Basic Form II

31

Crown

1. Fold Basic Form II (see page 31) with the front view faceup.
2. Fold diagonally.
3. Sharpen the fold well.
4. Pull out corners A and B from the inside, and you have a crown fit for a king or queen.

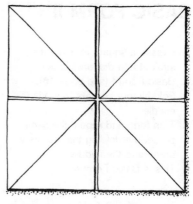

1 Front view, Basic Form II

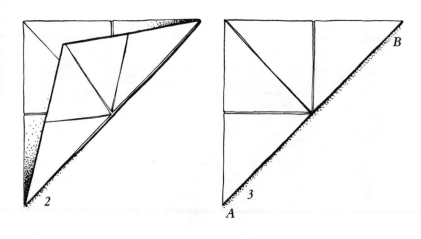

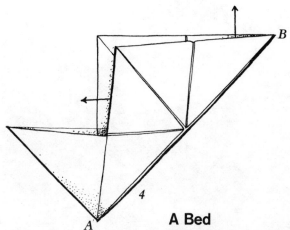

A Bed

The crown can be converted into a bed by folding the points in the middle to the inside.

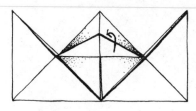

Crown

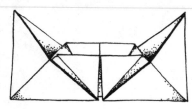

Bed

Salt-and-Pepper Dish or "Fortune Teller"

1. Fold Basic Form II (see page 31), with the front view faceup.
2. Lift the form off the table and start pulling the center-point corners up, as the outside corners move down.
3. Proceed with one point at a time as each opens to form a compartment. (Continued on next page.)

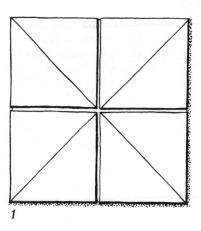

1

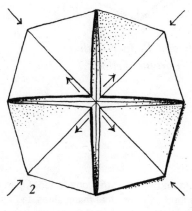

2

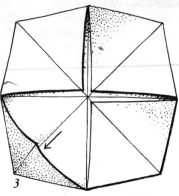

3

4. You now have four compartments
   in your dish for salt and pepper
   or, if you like, for other goodies.

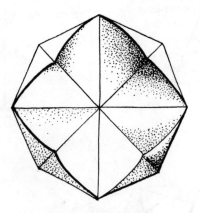

*4 Salt-and-Pepper Dish
or "Fortune Teller"*

"Fortune Teller"

If you turn the "dish" around and reach with four fingers into the compartments, you can open and close the form in two directions. Then you can play games by writing messages under the inner flaps and letting your friends pick a number from one to ten. Open and close that many times and ask them to pick left or right, or up or down, to find the flap that will reveal their fortune. (See photo on opposite page.)

Fish

1. Fold Basic Form II (see page 31) with the front view faceup.
2. Fold one corner towards the middle.
3. Fold the remaining corners to the middle, and . . .
4. . . . turn form over. Reach into the open diagonal, open . . .
5. . . . and then fold that section flat as shown. (Continued on next page.)

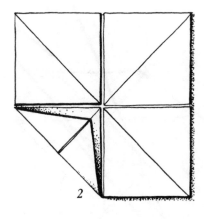

1

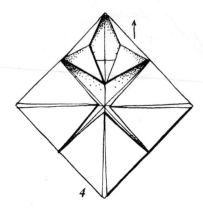

2

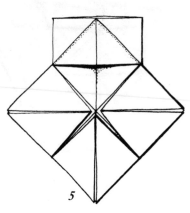

3

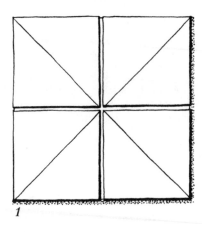

4

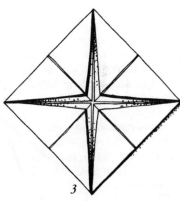

5

6. Do two more sections and flatten all folds with your thumbnail. Now you have a fish with a tail and fins.

All you have to do is give your fish an eye and maybe some other pretty markings (see page 38).

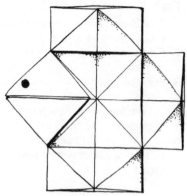

6 Fish

Steamboat

7. To make a steamboat fold the tail back to its previous position to match the fish's head.
8. Now reach under these two sections at the middle at points A and B. Push these into the outer corners while the form folds inward along the middle crease . . .
9. . . . and the two smokestacks— the former fish fins—come up to meet in the middle. Press the bow and stern folds with your thumbnail.

Dress up your steamboat with a whiff of cotton, draw on portholes or an anchor, or paint it a bright color.

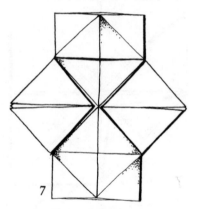

7

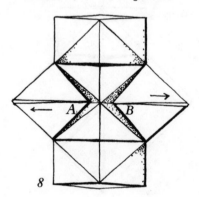

8

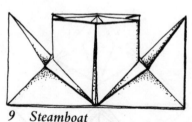

9 Steamboat

A Medal

Follow the description for the fish (pages 39 and 40) through Step 6 but open, fold, and flatten out all four corners. Use your imagination and decorate your "medal" with pretty colors.

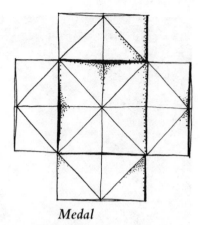

Medal

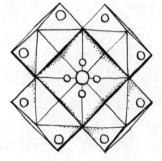

Furniture

You can make furniture for your dollhouse using the form for the medal above. If you fold three sections down and one up, you have a chair. Bend down all four, and there you have a table.

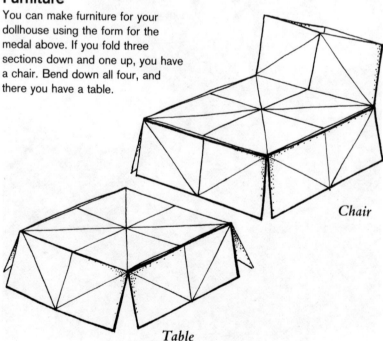

Chair

Table

BASIC FORM III

1. Crease a square to give you a straight cross.
2. Fold all four corners to the middle. Take the two corners A and B and...
3. ...fold the square in half. (Continued on next two pages.)

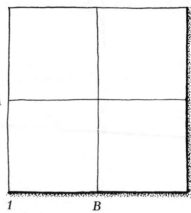

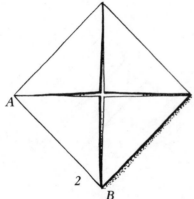

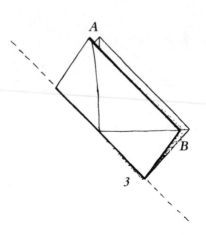

Basic Form III (continued)

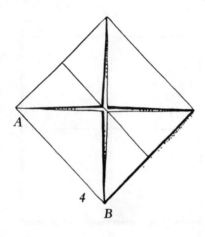

4. Open up the form.
5. Take up the corners A and B again and fold that edge to the midline crease. Do the same with the opposite corners. You now have a narrow, long rectangular form.

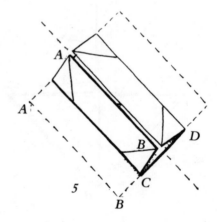

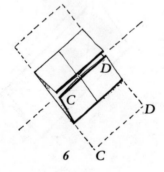

6. Now fold the corners C and D to the midline crease, and do likewise with the other half to again have a square form. (Continued on next page.)

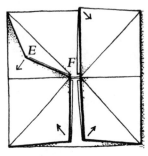

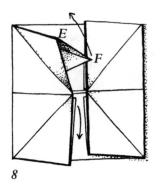

7 *Enlarged view relative to Step 6*

8

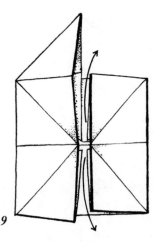

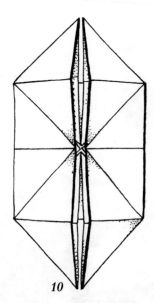

9

10

Basic Form III

7. Turn the square on the table so that the edges folded to the middle are vertical. Fold corner E diagonally to the midline. Repeat with the remaining corners.

8. Now pull tip F, which is hidden under corner E, out while holding the form at the right side.

Sharpen the hidden diagonal crease.

9. Repeat Step 8 with the remaining corners.

10. This is Basic Form III, which is the basis for many more difficult forms.

Catamaran

1. Fold Basic Form III (see pages 43 to 45).

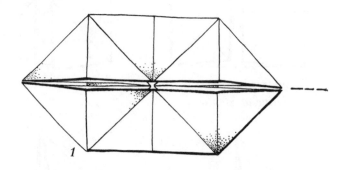

2. Fold the top portion of the form backwards along the middle crease.
3. Gently pull both halves apart and you will have a catamaran.

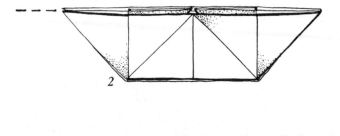

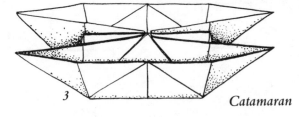

Catamaran

Catamaran with Sail

4. Hoist the sail by pulling the triangle in the center of one of the halves out, and you will have your sail.

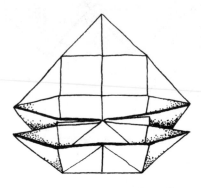

4 Catamaran with Sail

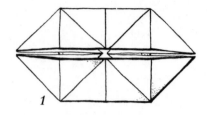

1

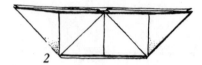

2

Purse or Wallet

1. Fold Basic Form III (see pages 43 to 45).
2. Fold the upper portion backwards along the middle crease.
3. Pull out the hidden triangle from the inside of the back portion.
4. Repeat Step 3 with the triangle in the front portion. Now fold the corners A, B, and C to the middle.

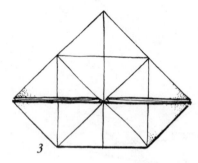

3

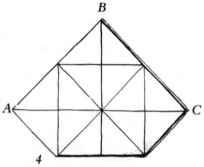

4

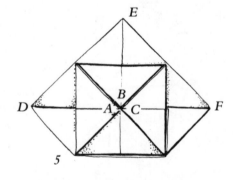

5

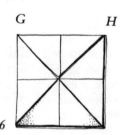

6

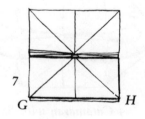

7

5. Fold the corners E, D, and F of the back portion rearward to the middle.
6. You now have a square.
7. Fold points G and H on the top portion of the form down to the bottom corners.

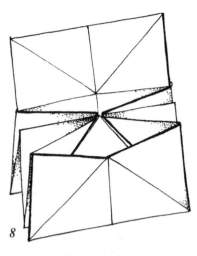

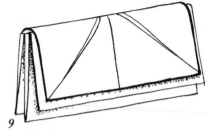

8. Reach into the inside and gently open your new purse or wallet.
9. The portion extending above is the flap.

Open Purse or Wallet with Flap Closed

Little Box

Open the flap of the purse or wallet. Reach inside each compartment and gently pull the form apart so that the divider becomes the bottom of the container. Pull out the sides and you have a little box for candies.

Gondola

1. Fold Basic Form III (see pages 43 to 45).

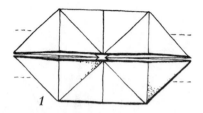

2. Fold the upper and lower portions rearward to meet at the middle crease.

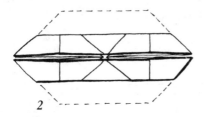

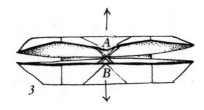

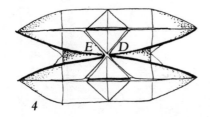

3. Reach inside and open up the form at points A and B.

4. Open the pockets and flatten all folds in the middle area but not at either end to the left or right. Pull out the corners C and D from the middle ...

5. ... so that they are upright, and then flatten them outward. Fold corners E and F outward. (Continued on next two pages.)

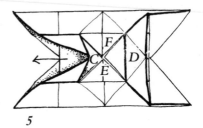

Gondola (continued)

6. Then carefully pull point E outward along the table surface. Grasp point F, and...

7. ...carefully do the same with the opposite side.

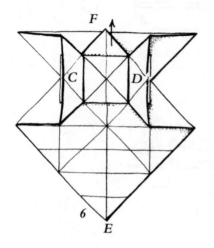

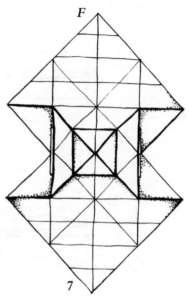

8. Turn form as shown. Fold the corners G, H, and J to the upper center, and the corners K, L, and M to the lower center.

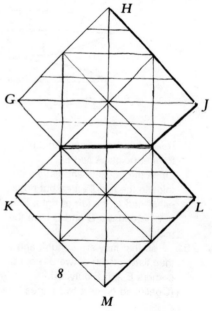

9. Now fold the upper and lower halves, N and O, respectively, in half.
10. Fold this form vertically to the right as shown.

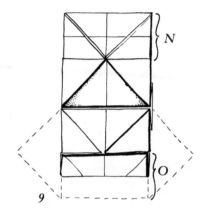

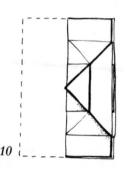

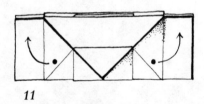

11. Turn the form horizontally and firmly grasp with the thumb and index finger of each hand at the points marked in the diagram. Slowly and carefully pull outward to unfold the gondola.
12. Now give the gondola its proper shape by tidying up the bow and stern, straightening the hull and sides, and flattening the middle passenger well.

12 The gondola

THE RECTANGLE

From a rectangular piece of paper you can fold many wonderful forms like a hat or helmet, a rowboat, or an airplane that flies. Typically the size as well as the shape of the paper is different than what we used for most of the previous forms. Here you can use writing paper, newspaper, paper from magazines, and especially giftwrap. Again, for smaller forms you might want to use origami paper. If you make your own, just make sure that the edges are perfect right angles.

The basic form for folding with rectangular paper is the straight cross, just like the one used with square paper.

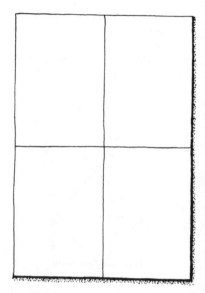

Rectangle

Hat

1. Crease the paper to get a straight cross and fold in half by folding down the upper portion at the midline.
2. Fold the upper right corner down along the vertical midline.

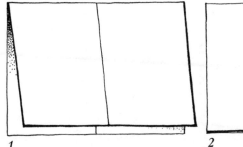

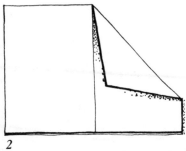

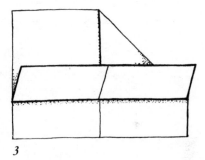

3. Fold up the portion extending at the bottom. Turn form over.
4. Repeat Steps 2 and 3 on this side and you have a hat.

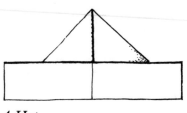

4 Hat

Helmet

To make a helmet just fold the corners of the hat down on both sides as indicated. (See page 55.)

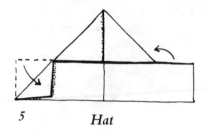

5   *Hat*

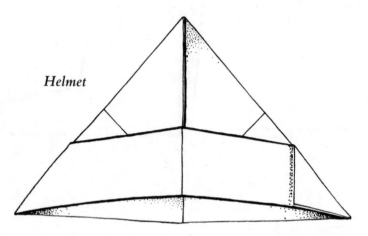

Helmet

Pyramid

1. Fold a helmet.
2. Open the form by pushing points A and B together . . .

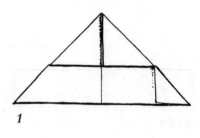

1

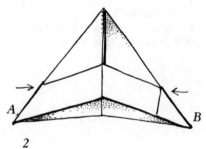

2

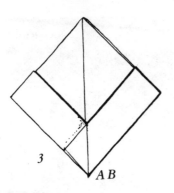

3

A B

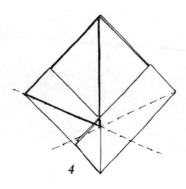

4

3. ...until these two points touch
   and the form is flat and square.
4. Following the marks in the
   diagram fold the faceup corner
   inside with two folds so that the
   distance along the middle crease
   to the new fold is equal to the
   length of the original edge of the
   form—an isosceles triangle.
5. Turn the form. Repeat Step 4
   and you have a pyramid. You can
   decorate your pyramid, if you like,
   and transform it into a tepee.

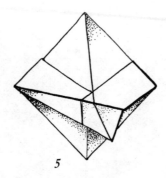

5

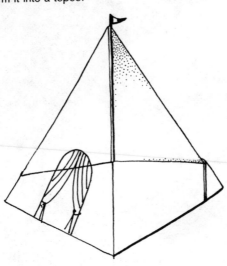

Rowboat

1. Fold a helmet (see page 56). Open the form by pushing the points together until the points touch and the form is flat and square.
2. Fold the faceup section in half by bringing the lower portion up flush with the top.
3. Turn form over. Repeat Step 2.

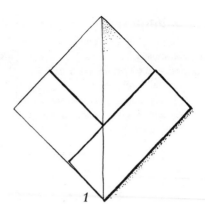

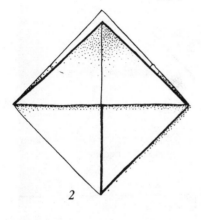

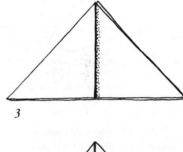

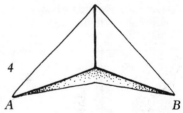

4. Open the form by pushing points A and B together so that they touch and the form is again flat.
5. With a flat side towards you hold the form at points C and D, and gently pull them apart. (Continued on next page.)

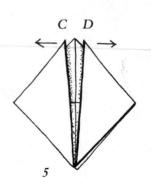

(continued)

6. The boat is appearing. Continue unfolding...
7. ...and fold both sides flat against each other.
8. Gently pull up the bow and stern by bending the bottom and you have a rowboat.

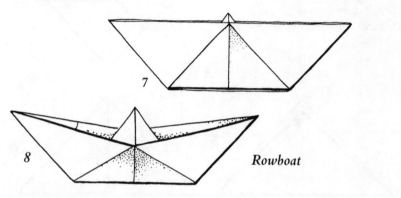

Rowboat

Airplane

1. Crease a rectangular piece of paper vertically and fold both lower corners to the midline.

2. Fold both of the diagonal edges against the midline.

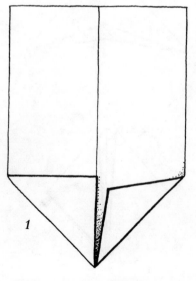

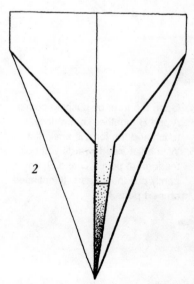

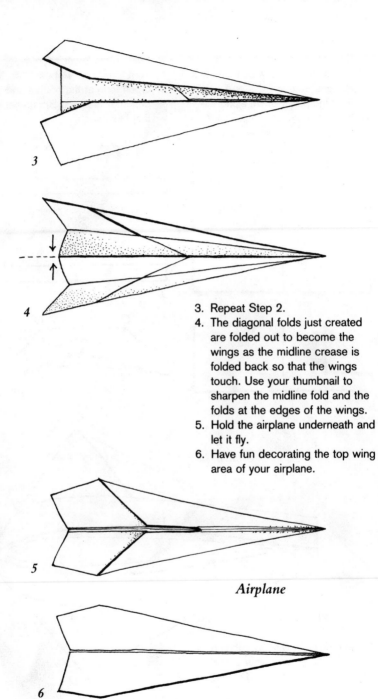

3. Repeat Step 2.
4. The diagonal folds just created are folded out to become the wings as the midline crease is folded back so that the wings touch. Use your thumbnail to sharpen the midline fold and the folds at the edges of the wings.
5. Hold the airplane underneath and let it fly.
6. Have fun decorating the top wing area of your airplane.

Airplane

Snatch-Jaw

1. Crease a rectangle oriented horizontally lengthwise to show a straight cross.
2. Fold the paper down along the horizontal crease. Then fold down both upper corners as shown.
3. Fold up the lower edge.
4. Turn form over. Repeat Step 3.
5. Open form at the bottom and push points A and B together so that they touch.

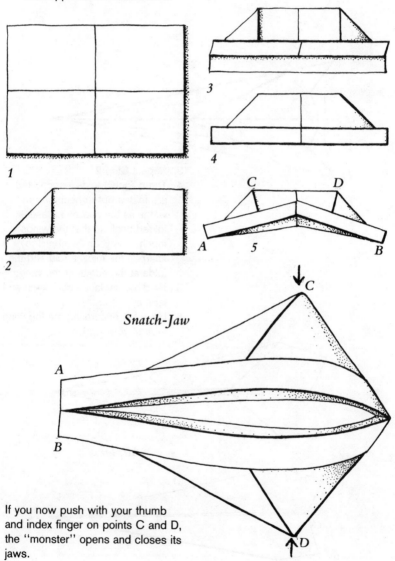

Snatch-Jaw

If you now push with your thumb and index finger on points C and D, the "monster" opens and closes its jaws.

VARIATION ON A BASIC FORM

Small Boxes

Small boxes have so many uses that it almost seems as if one can never have enough of them. Boxes can be folded in many different sizes and made out of many different materials. Here we show you how to make them with or without a lid, or transformed into a basket. With a little imagination you can paint designs on them or dress them up any way you like. It is also fun to make a whole set of nested boxes that fit snugly one inside the other.

A Square Box

1. Crease a square piece of paper to show a diagonal cross.
2. Fold all four corners to the middle.
3. Open up the form.
4. Fold each of the four corners to the opposite crease you just made. Open up the form again.
5. Fold each of the corners again but this time only up to the crease nearest to the corner. Open up the form.
6. With a pair of scissors cut into the "net" where marked with the dashes and extra heavy lines.

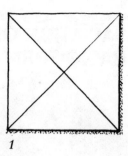

1

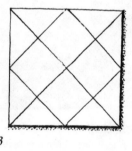

2

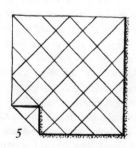

3

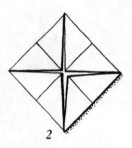

4

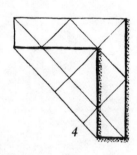

5

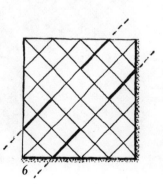

6

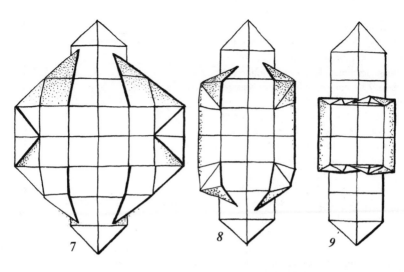

7

8

9

7. Turn the form on the table as shown and fold the left and right corners once.
8. Fold the left and right sides towards the middle one more time.
9. Bring both of these sides vertically upwards and fold the free edges in as shown on the diagram so that there are four upright sides.
10. Fold the upper and lower corners inward and fold each portion upwards at the base of the sides. Then fold them inside over the side.
11. Sharpen all folds to give the box stability.
12. An alternative for Steps 10 and 11 is to fold the upper and lower portions upright leaving the corners unfolded, and *then* fold them over the sides so that the corners cover the bottom of the box.

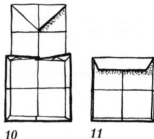

10

11

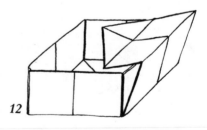

12

If you want the box to have a lid, repeat all steps but start with a piece of paper that is slightly larger. You can also make a basket out of the box of course by attaching a handle. Decorate your creation to your heart's content.

A Simple Box

This box is not quite as sturdy as the previous square box but it is a lot easier to make. This construction is equally as easy to make from square or rectangular paper.

1. Fold sides according to the form in the diagram. Start by creasing all four sides just in from the edges. Make the second inner crease according to how high you want the finished box to be.

2. Fold two adjacent sides upright and fold the square corner between sides in half. Position the folded corner against the side wall. Repeat for each side and corner.

3. Now fold the top edge over and glue to the insides.

For the lid make a box that is a trace larger with somewhat shorter sides.

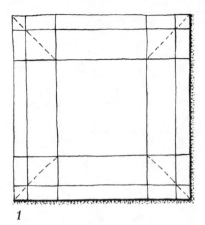

1

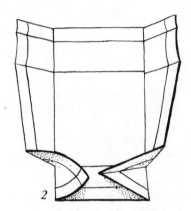

2

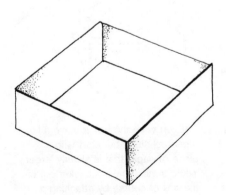

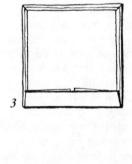

3

A Simple Box

66

Rectangular Box

1. The creases you need to make are shown in Diagram #1; choose distances that are appropriate for the size of the box you have in mind.
2. Fold along the narrow sides at points A–A. Open up the form to give creases.
3. Fold along both long sides at points B–B and a second time at points C–C.

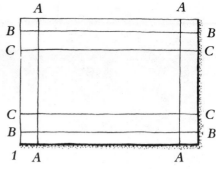

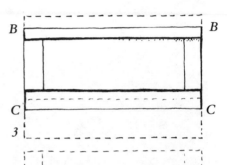

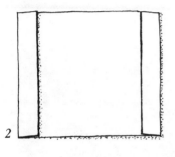

4. Now fold over the second fold on the long side (C–C) to the outside to become D–D. Turn form over and fold the corners inside as shown.
5. Now open corners upwards as shown by arrow and push the narrow sides upright. Finish by sharpening folds and flattening the narrow sides.

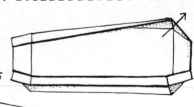

Rectangular Box

67

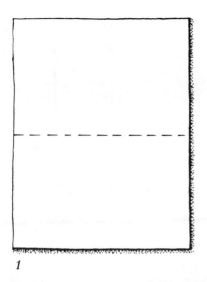

1

Drinking Cup

Use a paper that will not disintegrate as it is used, such as foil or foil-coated gift wrap.

1. You need a rectangle about the size of writing paper.
2. Fold the paper upwards in half as shown.
3. Fold up both corners A so that you still have a space about the width of your thumb between the corners. The midline is indicated for reference; don't crease the form along the midline.
4. Fold down the upper front edge.
5. Turn form over and fold the left and right ends to the middle.
6. Fold down the remaining upper edge.

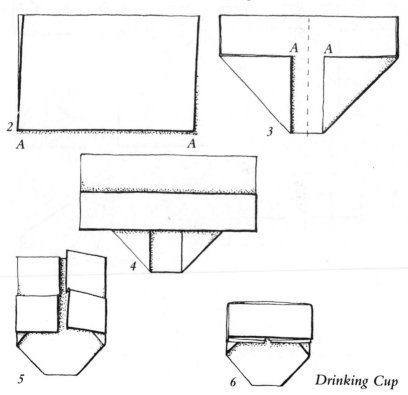

Drinking Cup

File Folder

1. Crease a rectangular piece of paper to show a straight cross.
2. Fold all four corners to the vertical midline.
3. Fold both points A to points B.
4. Fold the upper and lower portions to the middle.
5. Turn form over.
6. Fold both ends inward so that they touch in the middle.

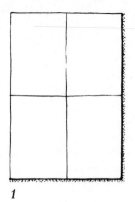

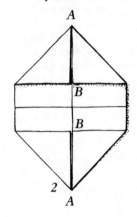

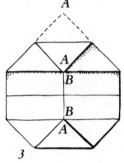

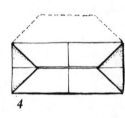

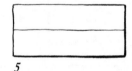

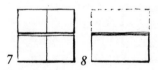

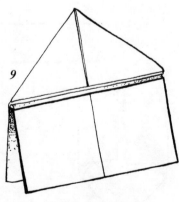

7. Turn form over again.
8. Fold the form in half by folding the upper half backwards to meet the lower half.
9. You now have two compartments. Pull the triangular portion out of one of them to create a flap for the folder.

File Folder

Party Hats

Every children's party—a birthday party, perhaps, or Halloween party—would not be complete without party hats. And you can make them yourself without much fuss. Decorated with bright colors and fun accessories, they add to the enjoyment for all. Newspaper or giftwrap is the best choice for this project. You already have one hat—a plain hat that can become a helmet (see page 54)—that you can modify into a party hat. Here we give you some additional suggestions to choose from.

Bishop's Hat

1. Start to fold a helmet from a rectangle (see page 54) but fold both of the upper corners to the same side, towards the front,

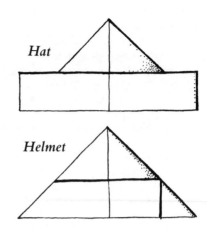

Hat

Helmet

before you fold up the portion extending at the bottom.
2. Turn form over and fold the right side to the middle.
3. Fold the left side to the middle.
4. Fold the bottom edge up and your hat is finished. This is the backview of the hat.
5. Turn form over for the front view.

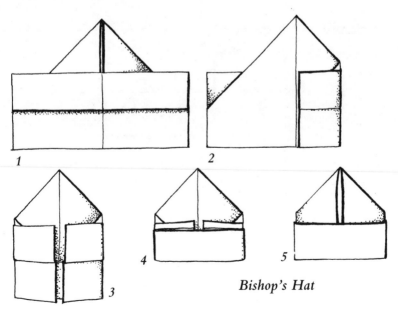

Bishop's Hat

71

Dutch Hat

1. You need a large rectangle approximately the size of newspaper or a sheet of gift wrap.
2. Fold the paper in half bringing the top edge down to meet the bottom edge.
3. Fold both upper corners down so that you have a distance between both the folds of about the length of your index finger.
4. Fold up the bottom edge.
5. Turn form and repeat Step 4.

For stability you might want to staple both sides together at either end. Don't forget to decorate your hat!

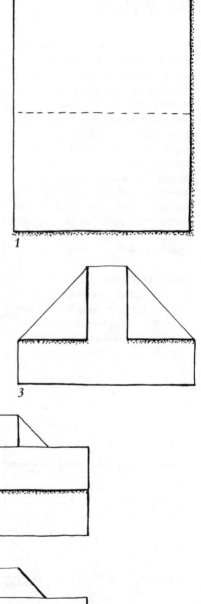

1

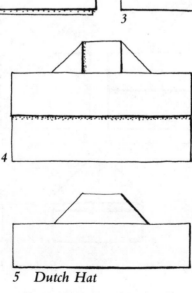

2

3

4

5 *Dutch Hat*

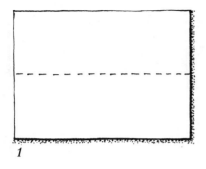

1

Beret

1. You need a large rectangle, but somewhat smaller than the one needed for the Dutch Hat.
2. Fold the paper horizontally in the middle.
3. Fold down both corners towards the middle but leave a small bottom edge exposed.
4. Fold up the edge of the faceup portion.
5. Turn form over and fold to the front both "wings"—indicated by the dashed line.
6. Now fold up the bottom edge as well. For decoration you might want to attach a feather to your creation.

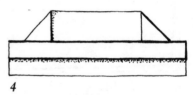

2

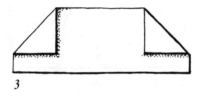

3   4

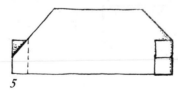

5

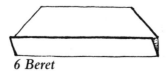

6 Beret

Mandarin Cap

1. You need a piece of paper approximately the length of that used for the Dutch Hat (page 72) but a bit narrower.
2. Fold the paper horizontally in the middle so that the upper edge comes down to meet the bottom edge.
3. Fold both upper corners diagonally to the midline as shown.
4. Fold up the bottom edge.
5. Turn form and fold the right and left ends or "wings" to the front.
6. Fold up the bottom edge and turn the form. This is your Mandarin Cap.

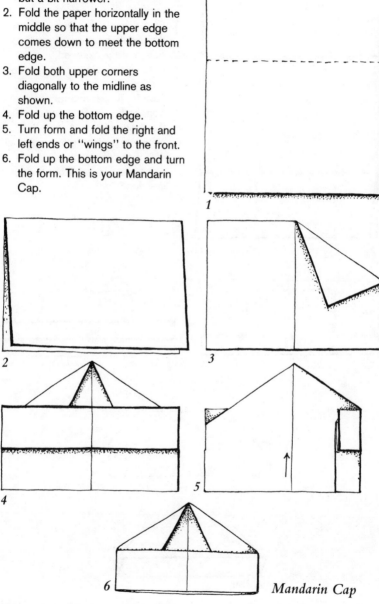

1

2

3

4

5

6   *Mandarin Cap*

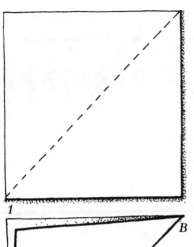

Turkish Fez

1. Start with a large square piece of paper—with each side about equal to the length of the piece used for the Dutch Hat (page 72).
2. Fold the paper diagonally as shown.
3. Fold up corner A so that it will become a triangle as shown.
4. Fold corner B down to corner C.

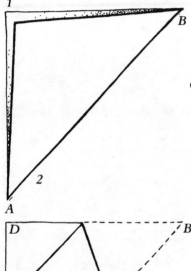

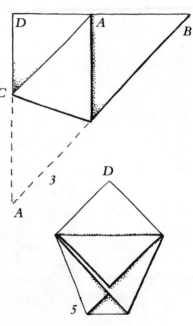

5. Turn form and fold down corner D of the faceup portion.
6. Fold the facedown portion backwards.
7. Rotate the form bottom edge up and here you have your Fez. To make it a true eastern Mediterranean hat decorate it with a tassle.

Turkish Fez

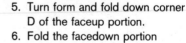

75

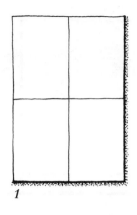

Noisemaker

The noisemaker is a fun toy for getting attention!

1. Crease a rectangle to show a straight cross.
2. Fold all four corners to the vertical midline.
3. Fold form in half to the right along the vertical midline.
4. Fold corner A up to the horizontal midline.
5. Fold corner B down to point A.
6. Fold form in half backwards.

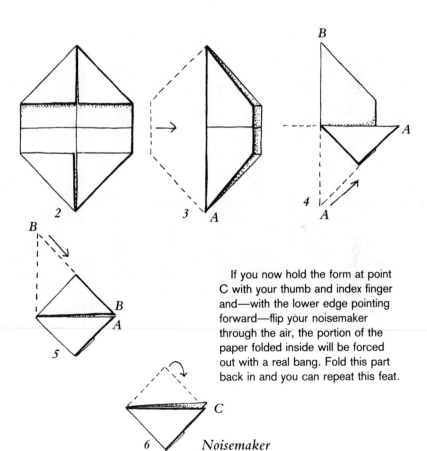

If you now hold the form at point C with your thumb and index finger and—with the lower edge pointing forward—flip your noisemaker through the air, the portion of the paper folded inside will be forced out with a real bang. Fold this part back in and you can repeat this feat.

Noisemaker

Double Noisemaker

1. Crease a rectangle to show a straight cross.
2. Fold all four corners to the vertical midline.
3. Fold form in half backwards along the horizontal midline.
4. Fold the upper right corner down to the midline as shown. Do the same with the upper left corner.
5. Open up the form.

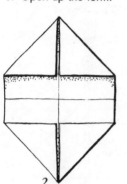

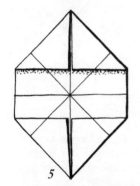

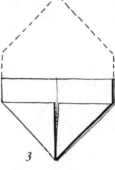

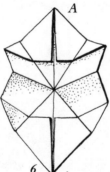

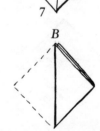

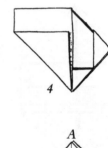

6. Fold form—as shown—at the creases so that both halves of the horizontal midline fold up to meet and then points A close the form to touch.
7. This gives you two compartments.
8. Now fold the form in half along the crease.

8 Double Noisemaker

Hold the form tight at corner B and listen to its double "bang."

78

MORE DIFFICULT
FOLDING FORMS

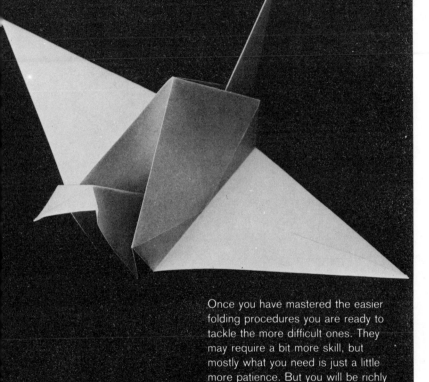

Once you have mastered the easier
folding procedures you are ready to
tackle the more difficult ones. They
may require a bit more skill, but
mostly what you need is just a little
more patience. But you will be richly
rewarded. Imagine! You can create
a bird in flight, a stork or a raven,
and a frog, and each form starts out
with a flat piece of paper. You can
even make a wonderful butterfly
collection or collect a group of
animals that any zoo would be proud
to have.

A Bird in Flight

1. Crease a square to show the straight and diagonal cross.
2. Fold up the bottom left corner to the diagonal crease as shown. Open up the form.
3. Repeat Step 2 for each corner in both directions along each diagonal.

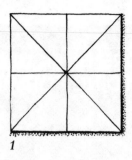

1

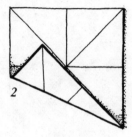

2

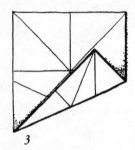

3

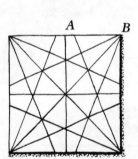

4

4. Open up the form. This is the "net" that gives you all the necessary creases. Fold corner B inside along crease A—A...
5. ...and follow this by folding point B to point C.
6. The form should now correspond to the diagram below.

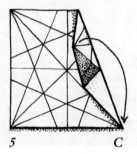

5 C

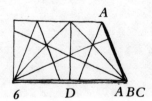

6 D A B C

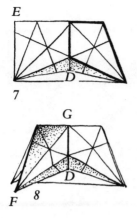

7

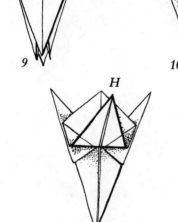

8

7. Push up the lower edge at point D; this way you have created a rhomboid (see the dark outlined area on the right side of the diagram). Open the form slightly and bend corner E inside.

8. Bend in the rhomboid on the left along its midline F—G; fold it together and push it under the right rhomboid.

9. Fold the back portion in the same manner to produce the form shown in the diagram.

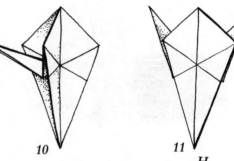

9   10   11

H

12

H

10. Pull out one of the points hidden within.

11. Pull out the other hidden point and you now have the head and tail of the bird.

12. Fold up corner H; this triangle is a wing.

13. Repeat for the other side. Shape the left point to create the head and you have your bird in flight.

13 Bird in Flight

Butterfly

1. Crease a square to show the straight and diagonal cross. Press all the folds well so that the creases are sharp.
2. Lift the upper corners and fold the form in half horizontally while pushing each half of the middle crease with your index fingers from underneath so that they meet. As the form flattens it will have a triangular shape resting on top of another triangular shape with an internal fold between each as shown.
3. Fold corners A and B up to point C.
4. Crease corners D and E first from the base to the midline, and then from the point to the midline.
5. Hold points F and G each with thumb and index finger, and push the little triangles together towards the middle—sharpening the folds as points F and G become upright.

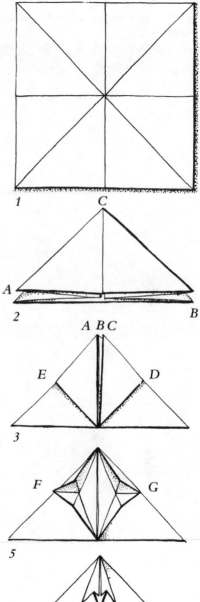

6. This is the underside of the butterfly, which you have just given feet. Turn your butterfly around and decorate the wings.

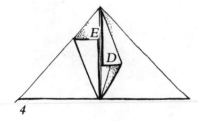

6 Butterfly

The Flying Swallow

1. Make a square from a rectangular piece of paper by folding the upper right corner over to the left edge. This gives you the square. The excess—cut off—gives you just the right portion to use for the tail of your swallow.
2. Make a butterfly (see page 83). Lay it on its wings, feet up.
3. Fold the upper portion back at the point of the small feet as shown.
4. Turn form over.
5. Fold form in half backwards as shown.
6. Pull out the inner section of both of the small protruding triangles—front and back of form—for the swallow's feet.

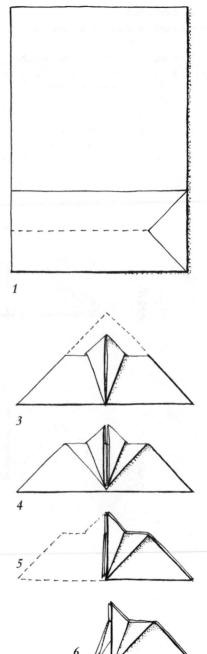

Now open the form to reveal the swallow wings, but leave the wings at an angle for proper flying shape. Take the left-over piece of paper you cut for the tail when you made the square and fold it in half. Cut a triangle off, cutting from the overlapping edges in towards the fold line. Open the tail and slip it into the form between the body and the wings. Now let your swallow really fly.

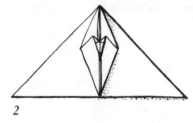

A Bellows

1. Fold a butterfly (see page 83).
2. Turn form over.
3. Fold both corners A and B up to point C.
4. Fold both corners D and E up and over to the midline.
5. Open up the folds of Step 4.
6. Fold corners D and E over and down to the midline. Open up these folds.

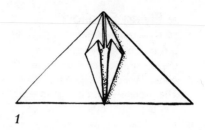

1

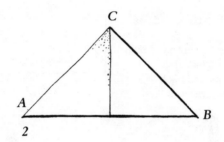

2

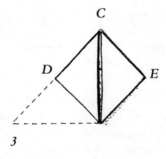

3

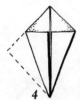

4

5

6

7. Hold form at points F and G and fold them together by squeezing from above and below while pushing towards the midline.
8. The diagram shows the side view of the form after you complete Step 7.

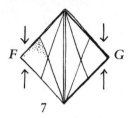

7

Hold bellows by both sets of tips and push it together to expel air. When you pull them apart again, air is sucked in.

You can also make a "devil's head" out of the form by holding on tight to the lower set of tips and blowing air in until the two upper extensions pop out like horns.

8

Bellows

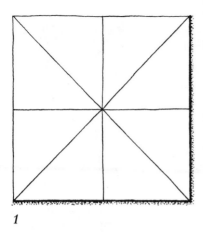

1

Stork in Flight

1. Crease a square to show the straight and diagonal cross.
2. Fold the form into a small square by pushing each half of the diagonal creases inwards to meet at the middle. (For comparison, see also page 83, Step 2).
3. Fold the corners A and B up to the midline.
4. Fold corner C down into a triangular shape.
5. Open up Steps 3 and 4. Now pull at point D to open the form...(Continued on next page.)

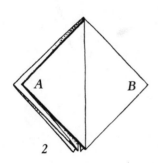

2

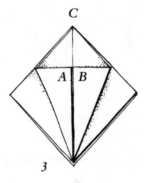

3

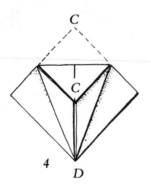

4

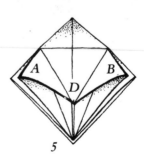

5

Stork in Flight (continued)

6. ...and continue pulling this lower point upwards to bring points A and B to the midline as shown.
7. Turn form and repeat Step 6.

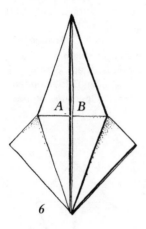

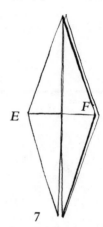

8. Fold point E to point F.
9. Turn form and repeat Step 8.
10. Fold points G and H to meet at the midline.

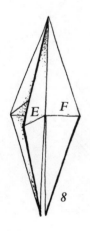

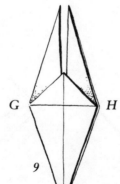

11. Turn form and repeat
    Step 10.
12. Fold point J to point K.
13. Turn form and repeat
    Step 12.

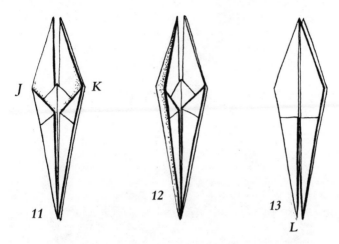

14. Pull point L upwards. The sides
    will open up a little. Push this
    extension slightly past the
    halfway point so that it slants
    towards the midline. Repeat on
    the right side.

Shape the head, tail, and wings to
give life to the stork in flight (see
photo, page 88).

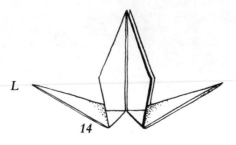

Stork in Flight

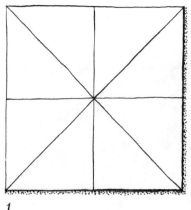

Raven

1. Crease a square to show the straight and diagonal cross.
2. Fold the form according to the instructions for the Stork in Flight through Step 9 (see pages 89 and 90).
3. Rotate the form to the orientation shown.
4. Fold form along the midline so that point A and B touch.

1

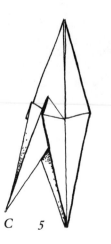

2

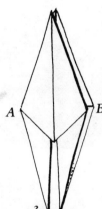

3

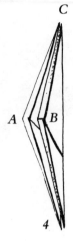

C

A *B*

4

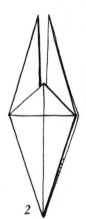

C *5*

6

5. Pull point C down as shown as you slightly open the form, making sure that the middle fold of this portion continues to face inward.
6. Close the form and fold head and feet as shown by the dashes. Pull the tail apart to give your bird a secure stance.

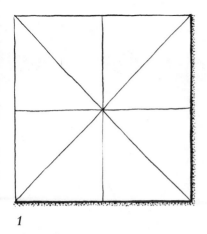

1

Frog

1. Crease a square to show the straight and diagonal cross.
2. Fold into a smaller square by pushing each half of the diagonal creases inward to meet at the middle.
3. Reach into pocket A and open slightly.
4. Push line A—A down to the midline to form a triangle.
5. Repeat Steps 3 and 4 for each of the pockets.
6. Fold corners B and C to the midline. (Continued on next page.)

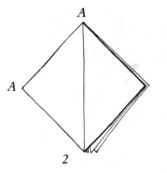

2

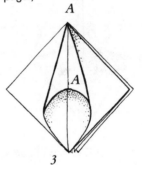

3

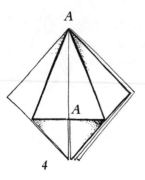

4

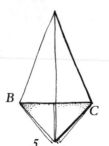

5

6

Frog (continued)

7. Unfold form and pull corner D upwards. The pocket will open up and corners B and C will move towards the midline.
8. Fold corner D up to the midline and the edges of corners B and C likewise to the midline. Flatten pocket. Repeat Steps 6, 7, and 8 for the other pocket.

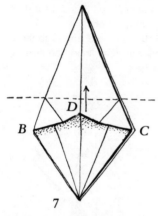

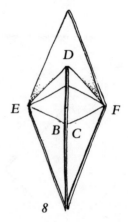

9. Fold corner E on top of corner F.
10. Repeat Step 9 with all corners.
11. Fold corner G and H to the midline.

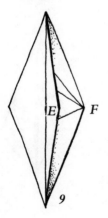

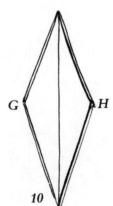

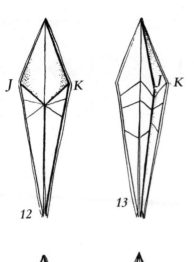

12. Repeat Step 11 with all corners.
13. Fold corner J on top of corner K.
14. Repeat Step 13 with remaining corners.
15. Pull point L upwards; the side will open up slightly. Push up a little at the middle of this portion to bend it backwards so that you can pull it out of the form as shown.
16. Repeat Step 15 with the three other points as shown. These are the front and back legs of your frog. Crease them for the proper appearance.

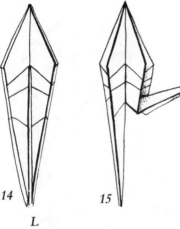

At the opening underneath you can inflate the frog. It may even leap if you press your finger gently on its back and release.

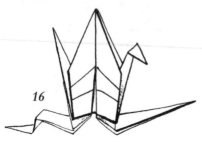

Frog

Umbrella

1. Crease a square to show the straight and diagonal cross.
2. Fold a small square by pushing each half of the diagonal creases inward to meet at the middle.
3. Reach into pocket A and pull it out a little.
4. Push line A—A down to the midline to form a triangle.
5. Repeat Steps 3 and 4 for each of the pockets.

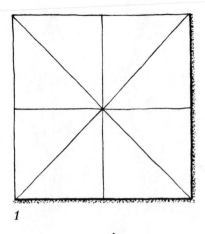

1

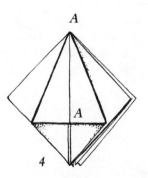

2

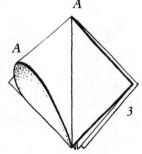

3

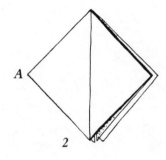

4

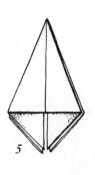

5

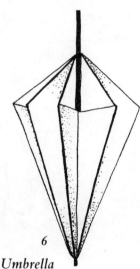

6

Umbrella

6. Fasten a stick to the inside; if it's a small table decoration, a toothpick is ideal. Unfold your "umbrella" to decorate it with your personal touch.

98

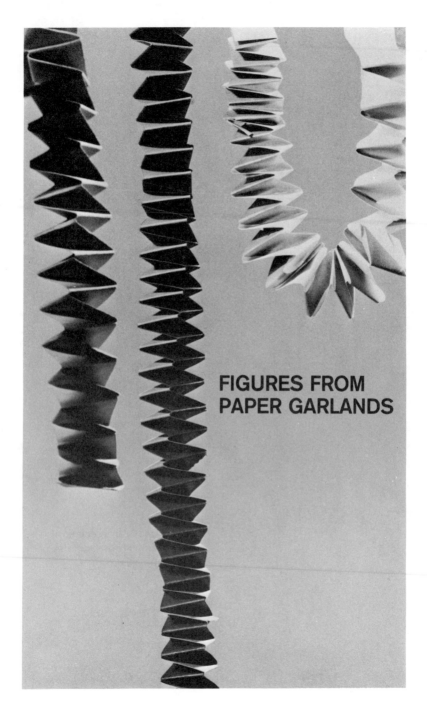

FIGURES FROM
PAPER GARLANDS

Cat-spring

If you fold two garlands of identical length together you have a "cat-spring." You can make both garlands out of the same paper or choose different colors. Your choice of paper is unlimited as long as the paper isn't too thin. For a trial run cut some paper into two matching, long and narrow strips and follow the steps.

1. Position piece A at a 90° angle to piece B.
2. Fold B from left to right over A.
3. Now fold A over B in the same way, always folding the upper piece over the lower.
4. This folding technique gives the steplike appearance to the garland.
5. Either one long garland . . .
6. . . . or many different-colored shorter ones can be glued together.

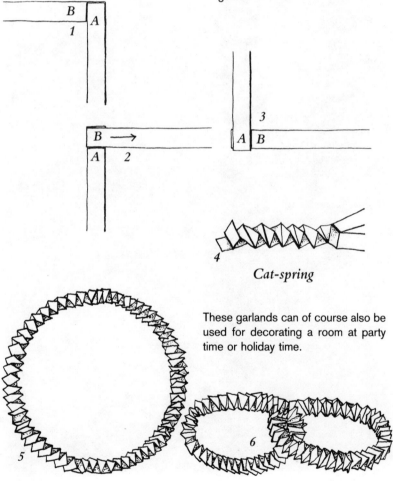

Cat-spring

These garlands can of course also be used for decorating a room at party time or holiday time.

Caterpillars, Snakes, Dragons, and Little Bugs

A piece of this garland simply decorated with dots or squiggles and two black dots for eyes is already a caterpillar.

Long pieces of garland that get smaller towards one end (cut paper accordingly) will make a snake.

A dragon needs a head with pointed teeth and a big tongue.

A little bug is happy with a very short piece of garland. All it needs is a head with antennae and little feet made from small strips of paper.

Snail

The snail requires a bit of patience. Fold two long pieces of paper four times wider on one end than the other into a garland. Now roll the garland to make the house that the snail carries on its back. If you thread a piece of wire through beforehand, the form will keep its shape.

The body of the snail is folded out of two pieces of paper that are about one and a half times as wide at the front end as at the tail end but widest in the middle. Again, wire will give the body its shape. Cut two small and narrow strips of paper for the antennae and glue the house in place.

The Cat

The "cat project" is a little bit more difficult. The best paper to use is probably brown wrapping paper or something of similar strength like paper grocery bags. Fold body and tail out of two long pieces of paper that are about twice as wide towards one end than towards the other. The pieces for the legs are about as wide as the tail.

The Cat

To give the body good shape and stability use thin wire—similar to that available from a florist—that can be pushed through the garland. With that kind of reinforcement your cat can really arch its back. The legs must be attached with glue. The last step is to attach the ears, and your project is complete.

Mr. and Mrs. Jumping Jack

Here is another easy and fun project to do with garlands. Using paper of many different colors you can create many figures of your own invention.

As another idea, here is a joyful Mr. and Mrs. Jumping Jack which we suspended on a string.

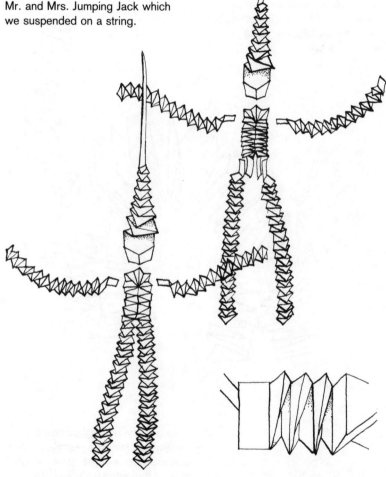

Jumping Jack

Again we used wire for reinforcement. Many other figures will lend themselves to this idea. Let your imagination guide you.

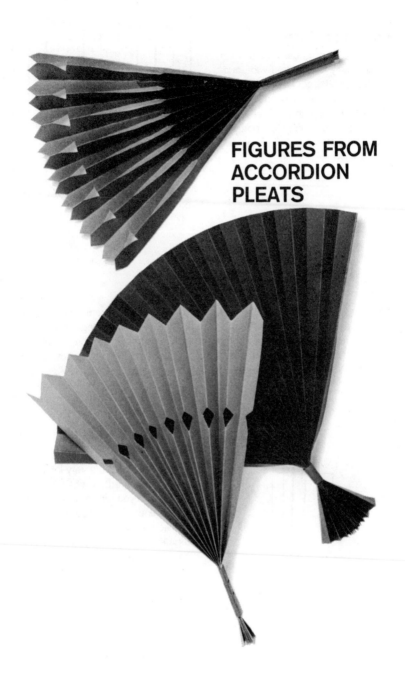

FIGURES FROM
ACCORDION
PLEATS

Making Accordion Pleats

Take a piece of paper that is considerably longer than wide and fold it in pleats, accordion-fashion. Here you have another basic form from which you can make all kinds of easy and fun things like butterflies and fishes, stars, and many other simple figures.

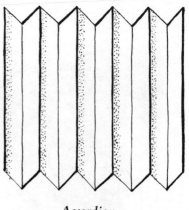

Accordion

Fan

You need a relatively long section to make a fan. Fold the fan tightly together and thread a string through one end, tying the ends tightly together. Now unfold evenly and you have a fan. By carefully cutting small triangles out at strategic places before unfolding you can create a wonderful design (see photo on previous page).

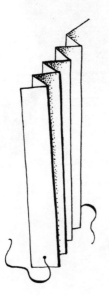

Star

This project needs a very long section of folded paper. Pull a string through as you did for the fan and tie the ends tightly together. In addition, fasten or glue the sides together, and you have a star. You can make your star especially pretty by making cutouts similar to the fan before you unfold the accordion fold (see opposite).

Dragonfly

The body of the dragonfly is a small roll of paper with narrowly pleated wings attached to it so that the pleats unfold vertically (see upper figure).

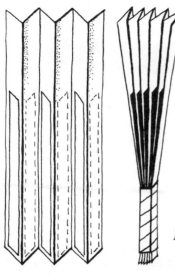

Fool's Wand

For the fool's wand you need a rather sturdy paper that is folded into very wide pleats. You can glue individual pieces of cardboard into one side of each pleat for added strength. The pleats should actually taper so that the lower third is slightly less wide for the handle. Wrap a pretty paper strip around the handle, gluing the beginning and the end in place.

Fool's Wand

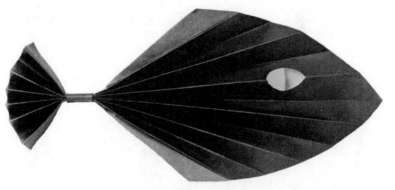

Butterfly

Fold a square into narrow pleats and tape the form in the middle to make two connected fan shapes. These are the wings. The body is made out of a roll of paper. You can tape or better glue it to the wings or better still cut a slit vertically through the center and slide the wings through the paper roll. Attach or cut out antennae on the end of the paper roll that is to be the head (see lower figure in photo opposite).

Fish

The fish can be made out of either a square or a rectangular piece of paper. Fold pleats and tie or tape a portion together on one end to form the tail. Cut the form to imitate a fish, and make a rounded cut for the eye as shown above.

Peacock

For the peacock you need two pleated sections and a body made out of sturdy cardboard. Copy the form for the body as shown, perhaps tracing it first with transparent paper and transferring it to the cardboard. You also might want to glue a piece of colored paper to the cardboard.

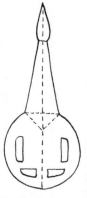

Pleated Wings

Cardboard Body

Crease the finished body along the dashed lines. Carefully cut out the slots for the tail and the wings. Pull the pleated wings through the slots and glue the tail pleats together.

GROUPING ANIMALS AND OTHER FIGURES TOGETHER

Many of the figures that we have seen how to make can be folded in different sizes. They can then be grouped together and wonderfully displayed in many fun ways. We give you a few suggestions in the following pages.

The Little Pig

1. Crease a square to show Net II (see page 18).
2. Fold together the upper and lower portions along the horizontal lines A—A so that they meet on the midline.
3. Bring the upper right corner down by lifting the middle right point B and bringing line B—B over to meet line C—B. Repeat for all corners.

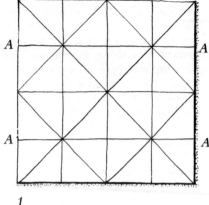

1

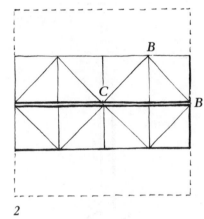

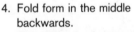

2

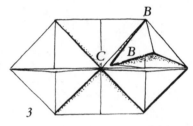

3

4

4. Fold form in the middle backwards.
5. Reposition the form so the open edge is on the bottom; fold out the triangles in the middle to make front and back legs as shown. Turn form and repeat.
6. Bend up the tip of the triangle on the right to form the head and snout. Paint eyes and curl the tail.

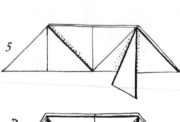

5

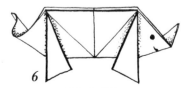

6

Little Pig

113

Evergreens and Bushes

Fold several helmets (see page 56). Arrange and glue them on top of each other as shown. For the tree trunk fold stiff paper or cardboard in half as shown. Make a stand for your tree by folding the ends of the trunk out and gluing a little strip of cardboard underneath as a crosspiece support.

You can use the form of the helmet by itself for bushes.

Use a big piece of green paper as grass; put a few pieces of hay around and some pieces of cut-up colored paper as animal fodder.

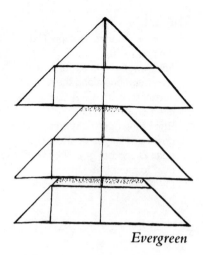

Evergreen

Trunk

Fence

If you now want to make a fence, cut strips of paper, fold over several times and cut out as shown for the post-and-rail style; put it around your barnyard and let your pig family have fun.

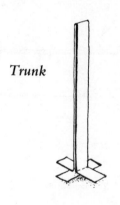

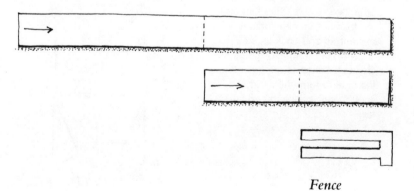

Fence

The Old Village

To build an old village you need houses of different sizes, a church, and trees. To keep the villagers safe, you need a wall, and your wall of course needs a gate. You can fold all of these things from paper and arrange and rearrange to your heart's content.

1

House

1. The basic form for a house needs a fairly small piece of paper, half as wide as it is long. Fold form in half.
2. Fold both upper corners to meet in the middle.
3. Unfold corners and fold them inside.
4. Fold vertical edges slightly forward; do the same with the bottom edge. Turn the form and repeat folding edges on that side.

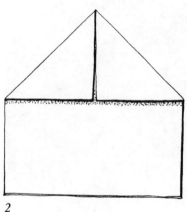

2

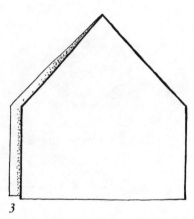

3

When you set up your houses, fold the edges inside. Windows and doors can either be cut out or drawn on.

House

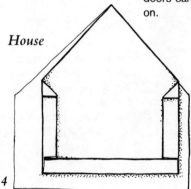

4

The Roof

1. For a roof you need a piece of paper that is twice as long as the height of the gable.
2. Fold paper in half and set it on top of the gable.
3. Fold the edges of the roof inside—following the outline of the gable—with great care.
4. As variation: cut a narrow strip of paper and glue it to the edge of the roof at the gable.

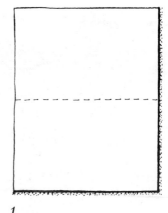

1

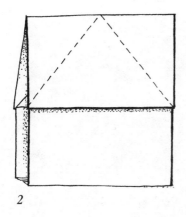

2

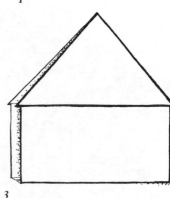

3

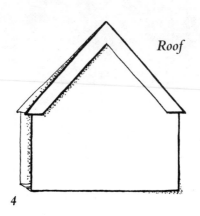

Roof

4

Here are some suggestions for village buildings with tall and pointed roofs (as needed for a church) or with flat-crested wide roofs. If the roof is very steep, you will want to cut off the corners at the gable that are normally folded in. Another way to make really old, old houses is by cutting the gable in step-fashion (see drawing below and photo opposite).

A church is constructed in two parts—the tower with steeple and the main body of the church—which are then joined.

An old city needed protection from outside forces and from the wilderness itself with a sturdy surrounding wall and a gate. The wall is made of a piece of paper that is folded in half with the lower edge folded inside to give it support. The wall can be shaped to the needs of the city. The gate is really a house without a roof—or even with one— and with a large opening cut out.

Trees

Trees are folded from green paper—
or other colors for autumn—pleated
in accordion fashion and then folded
in the middle. A strip of cardboard—
folded in half with the ends folded
out and a cross strip glued to form a
base—will make the tree trunk.

Open the top pleats of the tree's
crown and cut it to shape, if you
like. The round fan shape is formed
by making one cut with the pleats
folded together and then opening.

Bedouin Horsemen Riding in the Desert

Bedouin horsemen with their long, flowing capes ride through the desert. With a little imagination one can even see tents and in the distance an oasis with palm trees.

The Horse

1. Fold the bird (see page 27).
2. Open up slightly and fold down the tail to become the horse's head.
3. Fold point A of both wings over to the midline to make the horse's front legs.

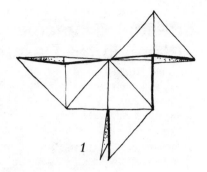

1

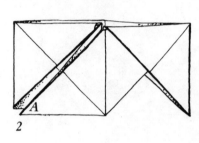

2

3

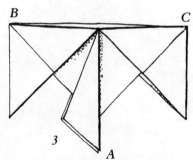

B

C

A

4. Fold back the horse's head by holding the form at points B and C and firmly pushing the head back into the form. Press these new interior folds. This puts the horse in an upright position.

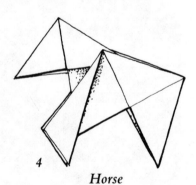

4

Horse

The Rider

1. Fold the vase (see page 25).
2. Fold down the second wing and push the middle third one in such a way that three wings are on top of one another.
3. Open up slightly and fold corner A over to the left side on the diagonal crease.
4. Fold this portion back halfway as shown.

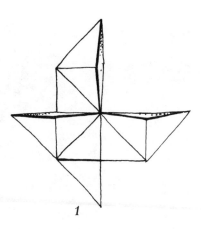

1

2

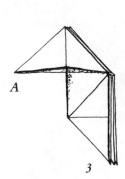

3

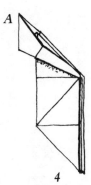

4

5. Now pull out the middle wing a little, flatten the form, and then open up a bit. Let the rider mount his horse, making sure that you push him gently but firmly onto his horse (see photo, page 121).

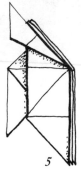

5

Rider

A Paper Doll

This little girl is all dressed up in a skirt, a short jacket, and a white apron. But if you like, you can change her into a colorful skirt and blouse. We will show you the basic forms from which you can "sew" your doll's clothes.

1. For all the clothes use the basic form for the medal with the four open and flattened corner pockets (see page 42).

The Blouse

2. Leave two pockets flat for the sleeves and open up the rest of the form. Fold the sides and bottom over to leave the crease pattern as shown.

The Skirt

3. Leave one pocket of the medal flat and open up the rest of the form. Carefully fold the sides and bottom edge over to display the creases shown. If you want a shorter skirt you can give it a hem by folding the form under some more along the bottom.

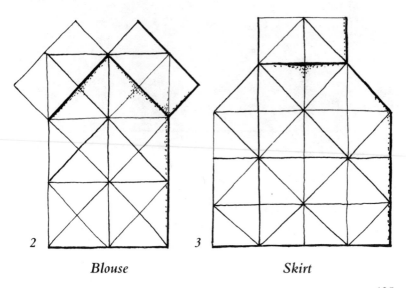

Blouse   Skirt

The Jacket

4. Flatten all four corner pockets of the medal and fold the form in half horizontally. You now have two sleeves. You can fold down both corners in the middle to make a collar.

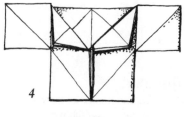

4

Jacket

The Apron

The apron is made from a very small piece of paper that is simply pleated. Attach a narrow paper strip to serve as the apron string.

All you have to do now to complete your doll is attach small paper strips to serve as arms and feet and give your doll a head. The head can also be made out of the form for the medal. Fold it in its appropriate size, paint a face, and add some hair—made from small paper strips or yarn. Give her a pretty paper ribbon bow and she is ready to play with you.

INDEX